If You Love Me,
Please Read This

If You Love Me, Please Read This

✦

A Challenge to the Men in Generation X
and Y from the People Who Love Them

*By Art Heemer
with Marilyn Wilson Miller
and Sharon Lilly Runyon*

iUniverse, Inc.
New York   Bloomington

If You Love Me, Please Read This
A Challenge to the Men in Generation X
and Y from the People Who Love Them

iUniverse books may be ordered through booksellers or by contacting:

iUniverse
1663 Liberty Drive
Bloomington, IN 47403
www.iuniverse.com
1-800-Authors (1-800-288-4677)

Because of the dynamic nature of the Internet, any Web addresses or links contained
in this book may have changed since publication and may no longer be valid.

ISBN: 978-1-4502-0582-5 (sc)
ISBN: 978-1-4502-0583-2 (ebk)

Printed in the United States of America

iUniverse rev. date: 2/16/2010

If You Love Me, Please Read This

A Challenge to the Men in Generation X and Y From the People Who Love Them

Your Mom
Your Wife
Your Girlfriend
Your Sister
Your Good Friend
Your Dad
Your Brother
Your Buddy

by
Art Heemer
with
Marilyn Wilson Miller and Sharon Lilly Runyon

Table of Contents

Acknowledgements

First, I wish to thank my two co-authors. Sharon Runyon and Marilyn Miller have both been friends of 35-plus years. I told them I would not do this project without them. They each have been excellent contributors to this book project. Sharon gave me the initial idea for this project and Marilyn has worked tirelessly to rein in my bombastic, revolutionary writing style. They will carry on this work admirably when I am gone.

Next, I wish to thank Ramona and Randy Severn for their contribution to the book. They have also been my friends for more than 35 years. Randy is a prime example of the Real Man, and Ramona is beyond reproach as a woman, wife, mother, and grandmother. I thank them for allowing me to include Ramona's reflection on Psalm 23, which was written during a low in their lives. You'll find it in the Prayer and Reflection section at the end of the book.

I also wish to thank all my pre-publication readers. Their comments and critiques have served to sharpen the focus of this book. In addition, thanks goes out to my good friend, Steve Rickey, for some legwork he did as I was researching this topic in the secular bookstores.

Special thanks go to Dr. Marilyn Prasun, who runs the Heart Failure Clinic at Memorial Medical Center, Springfield, Illinois. Her skills in the healing arts are the chief reason this book exists today. Competence, compassion, and comeliness are a killer combination. Thanks, Doc. You are way cool!

I dedicate this book to a certain young man in my life with whom I share a name. Maybe this will benefit him, too.

To the young men who read this little book: I hope you find the challenges we've raised are targeted to your life issues, and we hope you will grow in wisdom, strength, and resolve as Real Men. The world desperately needs your potential. Your women and children need your 'A' game.

If I don't see you here on earth, we'll meet in Heaven. I'll be at the buffet!

Arthur D. M. Heemer
B.A., M.A., M.Div., former pastor,
and fool for Jesus
August 29, 2009
Auburn, Illinois

1. Introduction:
There is a Problem

You see it in their eyes. When they look my way, I'm sure they're thinking, "I'm glad it's not my son." or, "What did they do wrong?" After all, it's what I might be thinking. How could things have gone so wrong with this child? The other kids are far from perfect, but well-adjusted, hard working, and living life. What did we miss? Did I not care enough, or too much? How can I reach this young man?

To the one who may be considering buying this for a young man as a gift:

There is a problem and it could end the society we have come to know and expect. Many of today's young men who are reaching the age of adulthood, estimated at 10 million in the U.S., seem to lack the training and skills necessary to be viable and vibrant Christians and productive, fulfilled citizens. Of course, I don't mean every young man is coping poorly with life, but we hear increasing commentary from worried parents, wives, girlfriends, siblings, friends, and employers about the fact that they know many young men whose lives seem to lack direction, focus, goals, motivation, and ambition. This trend is evident in the behavior, attitudes, beliefs, and values of these young men.

These are the young men of Generation X and Generation Y. Those in Gen X were born from the early 1960s through the late 1970s, while Gen Y came on the scene from the early 1980s through the late 1990s. Gen X is estimated to be a population of 23 million American males and Gen Y is estimated to be a population of 30 million American males. That is a pool of over 53 million young men of which 10 million are estimated to be affected young men and represent roughly 20 percent of this cohort. I am amazed at the number of people who claim that this estimate may be much too low!

So, what is the big deal with these men? What manifestations, attitudes, and behaviors do they exhibit, that would label them as dysfunctional? What is the commentary on a sizable portion of this cohort of young adults? The people they interact with on a daily basis, their family, friends, and employers, can best answer these questions.

It goes something like this.

"He's so gifted and full of such great potential, but he can't seem to stick to anything."

"He doesn't work and doesn't communicate with our family. He stays up all night on the Internet and sleeps all day."

"He can't hold a job, and it doesn't seem to bother him. We are out of answers."

"What turned my, once-cute little brother into this wreck of a man?"

"We grew up together. This is not the guy who used to protect me from bullies as we walked to school."

"We could just kick him out, but he might not survive."

"He is just drifting, as if his only goal is to make it through another day."

"His lifestyle and his professed claim to be a Christian do not match up. He's self-centered and only weakly committed to the kids and me. He gives the expected performance on Sunday and he's a mess the rest of the week."

"He's so troubled, but he won't talk to anyone. He'd rather self-medicate with excess food, alcohol, or drugs. I can't seem to make him understand how much I need him to step up and be the man of the house."

"We would promote him to a higher position in the company, but he lacks the values and discipline necessary for advancement. It's a shame."

These are examples of what parents, wives, sisters, friends, and employers say about the young men in their lives. We, the people who care about these young men, need to be asking some questions.

How did this happen?

Consider this. Young boys grow up and learn what is "normal" by observing the culture, adults, and situations they encounter around them. The TV and movies that young boys watch encode their attitudes, beliefs, and values for when they become men (attitude, belief, and value will be defined later). Do not think the funny TV shows depicting men as lazy, stupid, bumbling, shiftless, unproductive, valueless, never rewarded for gentleness, cold, distant, or glamorizing the player lifestyle aren't being processed by those young minds. These distorted portrayals of men are linked to humorous sitcoms; the messages are pleasantly viewed; and because children are rarely debriefed at the end of a night of TV watching, they tend to have an insidious effect.

Learning normalcy is also influenced by the presence or absence of intentional, instructional training and disciplined life lessons on the role of a man in society. The stresses of two parents working to keep families financially solvent combined with the shortcomings of latchkey realities, exhaustive after-school schedules, and weekend activities, leave limited time for quality training and nurture options. We are not passing judgment. It is what it is.

The Church should admit to some accountability here, too. Rarely do religious education programs intentionally develop curriculum to teach boys how to internalize and apply Christian principles and behaviors, as they become adolescents and adults interacting with the world. There are no "lab sessions," practicum experiences, or role-playing exercises to aid adolescents with the development of correct attitudes, beliefs, and values. These are the ways we train teachers, doctors, and lawyers in our culture. A former pastor I know has said that he felt these ways were too "worldly" for use in the Church. I think he is sadly mistaken. Just because a technique isn't expressly ordained in Holy Scripture doesn't really mean it couldn't be used effectively.

Church leaders who count warm bodies in the pews as evidence that they have fulfilled their mission to their parishioners, but who do not also invest in developing Christian men of strength and vitality, will see these men drift away. These young men will rarely achieve their God-ordained potential. The real tragedy in all of this is the loss of peace, joy, and fulfillment by these men and a continuation of the cycle of despair into the next generation will become increasingly probable. We grieve for these young men, for their families, for their troubled relationships with women, for their children, and for their careers. We grieve for the little children of the next generation, who view all this dysfunction as normal. Financial stability will erode and families will implode.

In most cases, loving parents, who respect each other and their children, seem to pass stable lifestyle values down to the next generation. Even so, a family can exhibit stable values and lifestyles, but a young person can still drift away. This book is not about affixing blame. Too many parents, wives, girlfriends, and others are engaged in that useless pursuit. Affixing blame is a fool's game, where no one wins and young men keep slipping away. Now is the time for doing, not blaming. Our prayer is that this little book can have a part in pointing your young man toward a vision of his true potential—his new beginning. You know him and realize what he could become with the correct guidance. We think a copy of *If You Love Me, Please Read This* will help him sort out some issues in his life and show him where he may be confused as to how to get his life pointed in the right direction.

Let's face it:

Our young men are where they find themselves due to countless variables (cultural, familial, situational, and individual), that have had an impact in their lives—the attitudes, beliefs, and values they internalized, and the choices they made about their priorities for living their individual lives. They have followed their individual free moral will and at some point they have made the decisions (or neglected to make decisions) that have placed them exactly where they find themselves today. We cannot even place the blame solely at their feet. These men have grown up in a world of dual-paycheck households with latchkey care structures. They belong to blended families with four parents and eight grandparents, who made sure the toy boxes were always well stocked. They have the latest high-tech gadgets and the lightening quick information capabilities of the Internet at their fingertips to satisfy an astounding instant gratification mindset, which is immersed in a post-Christian and increasingly secular culture where values and ethics are more fluidly expressed in cultural norms than ever before in this society. That is the demographic of this group. The traditional underpinnings of 1950s America are absent and may not return. These variables of material excess and spiritual minimization have given rise to behavioral manifestations of alienation and loss of motivation. Consequently, these young men are unsure of their intended role in life. There is quite enough accountability to go around.

So what happened?

Life happened. Parents do not always get the children they deserve. They are dealing with the adults those children have decided to become. Parents, loved ones, and concerned friends just want these young men to make a move toward growing up and accepting responsibility for their lives.

As we were struggling with what to say to encourage you to place this little book in the hands of your troubled young men, Marilyn Miller, one of my co-authors, had the best take on all of this when she stated:

"We have no blame to place here. We don't know all the whys, but we do know that God's plan for your young man—your son/brother/husband/boyfriend/friend/employee—is to live an abundant life. God promised that.

You are not alone. Thousands of other parents and concerned people in this country share your pain. If these pages help you, or help him in some way, then to God be the glory. We understand your love, concern, and pain; we understand your feelings of helplessness. We only seek to provide a first step for the young man in your life—to consider a step back from the cliff of no return. Perhaps this book will offer him a glimpse of a fuller life ahead."

This book was written to address a staggering need in the world today. Due to the phenomenon of young men who are unsure of their role as men, husbands, fathers, and productive citizens, the infrastructure of the family unit is being damaged. Young men who are not achieving their full potential are having a negative impact on the economy of their family units as well as the national economy. The trickle-down effect to the next generation is going to be exponentially worse if things continue without correction. The need is evident, urgent, and immediate. We must address this problem clearly, passionately, and forcefully.

What can be done?

We—Marilyn, Sharon, and I—have scoured the Christian resources for materials to place in the hands of the troubled young men we know, but we have found *nothing*! There are bits and pieces scattered throughout the secular shelves, but nothing exists in compact form with an overarching Christian worldview. This project was born out of that discovery. We hope you will give this book to a young man who holds the promise of great potential and achievement.

To the guys who receive this book:

We wrote this book to young men in an attempt to fill the gap between where you find yourself and what you might aspire to become. Our goal has been to be bold, but with the "churchliness" kept to a minimum. However, since you are reading this, you may see the words God, Jesus, and Holy Spirit thrown in occasionally. Do not panic! It will be okay. I maintain that help is often found in the craziest places. We are going to build on your foundation. We are going to strengthen that foundation and expand your vision of what you can really become as a vital, fulfilled man. You will learn, step-by-step, how to identify your unique growth issues and how to attack each one systematically. It is our prayer that this process will allow you to see God's vision for you, and that your vision of your true potential will interface with God's purpose for your life. We want you to see yourself clearly—your strengths and weaknesses—so you can begin to make the necessary adjustments as a man, boyfriend, husband, father, and valuable contributor in the business world, so that you will become all you were intended to achieve—capable of great things.

If you are not Christian:

We may be accused of neglecting young men of Jewish, Muslim, and other faiths, or even the agnostics who want more stability in their lives. While Christian young men are the primary audience for this book, those from other faith traditions and spiritual worldviews may find applicable thoughts for their unique issues and lives. As the Jewish folks say about chicken soup given for colds, "It couldn't hurt!"

Who is writing this book?

We are one man and two women doing this project. The man, Art, was a troubled young man, who found his way out of a dysfunctional childhood and into a committed Christian life and lifestyle. The two women, Sharon and Marilyn, have lived lives of purpose and commitment to their Christian values. All three of us know young men drifting through life who we hope might benefit from this resource. Sharon Runyon (also a co-author) has developed a women's ministry in Michigan, called Oasis. She interacts with the girlfriends, wives, and mothers of these troubled young men, who are painfully watching the young men they love live unfulfilled lives of dysfunction with little hope for a better future. Her initial idea and our discussions have lead to this book. Marilyn Miller has a long history of working with Christian organizations and interacts with young men and their loved ones.

We meet mothers and wives of young men who raise these issues on a regular basis. We see the pain in their eyes as they relate their concerns. We want to help the young men in these women's lives achieve their full potential. To this end, we have committed our training, our talents, and our resources. We are trying to help break some of the generational cycles that do such a disservice to young men in too many places.

So, strap in, guys; here we go!

2. What Gives Me the Right to Talk to You?

It's a valid question. I am about to tell you some very pointed things. You might even think I am speaking like an expert in the matter of troubled, abused, and dysfunctional young men.

I am an expert. Allow me to prove my point. I was such a troubled young man. I was born into a dysfunctional home. My mother lost the first baby she carried and blamed my father, who beat her regularly. They separated and divorced early in my life. She became a prostitute and wandered the country. I was given to my father. He was not up to the task of raising me. When my uncle, my father's eldest brother, came to pick me up "for a few days," he found a two-year-old eating a breakfast of moldy corn flakes and sour milk alone in the apartment. I am told I was left unsupervised quite a bit of the time. So, off I went to my uncle's home.

My uncle meant well, but he did not confer with his wife on the matter. She was already caring for five children of her own and was not thrilled to have another child in the house. I stayed in that home for fifteen and a half years. Those years were filled with psychological and physical abuse.

My aunt once tried to drown me as I was taking a bath. To this day, I do not know what triggered her action or what stopped her from killing me. I was about eight years old at the time. I can remember holding my breath, just looking into her eyes. She must have held me under for about twenty seconds. She suddenly let go and walked away. That day I began to believe in guardian angels. She and I never discussed the incident, but I pondered it often.

She viciously attacked with kitchen implements and publicly humiliated me often. She purposely underfed me as a teenager, and I was not allowed to sit with the family for meals. I had to eat in the kitchen standing at the counter. All the while, I mowed the grass, pulled the weeds, took out the trash, and shoveled the snow without being told. I would mow lawns in the summer and shovel driveways in the early mornings before school in the winter, but I was not allowed to keep any of the money. I put the money I earned in her hand and never saw it again, even though they were not a poor family—my uncle was a corporate president.

My aunt's anger lasted until I went to college. In high school, I was a good student. I was involved in the school choir, the speech and debate team, and I did some acting. I never missed school, because the worst day at school was better than any given day at home.

My downward slide began in college. I had earned a full scholarship to study at Indiana University in Bloomington, Indiana, and thought I would like to study pre-medicine. However, because I had been so abused and stifled as a teen I did not know how to handle my instant freedom. My grades plummeted and I flunked out. That dream was gone.

I struggled to live on my own and worked factory jobs to support myself, but I knew I was capable of more. One day, one of the cousins with whom I grew up uttered the magic words: "You are going to be just like your father." Those few words carried a depth of meaning for me: none of it positive, none of it good, and none of it well intentioned. My father was not a man who had developed his full potential—not by a long shot.

When my father was born, the attending physician accidentally pulled off his right arm at the shoulder. My grandmother catered to his every whim and babied him all his life, until her death. As a result, my father was self-centered and stunted socially. He never developed a good sense of responsibility, or a good work ethic.

My father was certainly no fool. He was above average in intelligence. He could play baseball with just the one arm. He played the trombone in the school band. He rode a specially designed ten-speed bike. Yet all he could aspire to was to become a cab driver and later a dispatcher for that cab company. He was offered college training, but he turned it down. His brother gave him a job in his accounting agency, but he would not go to work. He was a slacker before the term was invented. Those magic words, spoken by my cousin, galvanized me into action. My mantra became, "I'll show them!" I applied to a little college in Mishawaka, Indiana, named Bethel College, and entered in the winter term of 1971, on probation with a 0.89 grade point average (GPA). That is not even a D average! I was the editor of the college newspaper for three years and student body president my senior year. I was known as the "Campus Radical." I graduated in 1975 with a 3.60 GPA out of a possible 4.00, and earned the status of *magna cum laude*, which is Latin for "with great honor."

I then went off to West Virginia University in Morgantown, West Virginia, and earned a Master of Arts degree, with research thesis and a

3.81 GPA, in thirteen months. After that, it was off to Purdue University, in West Lafayette, Indiana, for a year of study on the Ph.D. level where I achieved a 5.11 GPA out of a possible 6.00.

I have had several good business opportunities and I have won awards for my business endeavors. Later in my life, I entered the ministry and earned another graduate degree, the Master of Divinity, with a 3.785 GPA, from Garrett-Evangelical Theological Seminary, on the campus of Northwestern University in Evanston, Illinois.

I am the only one in my biological family of three half-sisters and three half-brothers who has any college training. I am the only one in the family I grew up with who has an advanced graduate degree. I did show them.

I could have quite literally "gone to hell" because of my childhood experiences, but something got to my soul. My cousin did not mean me well when she uttered those words, but I turned them to good. I used them as a springboard to change my lot in life.

So, do not give me that old song about "Well, you're smart and gifted." My IQ is just above average, but I know the great secret. You see, I have the "make-up gene." I can make up for any deficiency with hard work, perseverance, and determination. I was willing to work awful, horrid jobs through the night so I could go to classes in the day. Some of my classmates would ask me to sit away from them because I smelled so badly after working all night around fetid and stinking industrial processing water, but that didn't bother me. I was happy for the chance even to be attending college classes. I wore old jeans and blue work shirts all through college, but that was okay. I did not care that the others dressed better. I was rescuing my life. I once worked in a brass foundry, where it was so hot my jeans would occasionally catch on fire at the bottom of my pant legs. The fumes were so bad from the processing of scrap metals there was always a thick haze at the furnace, and the smell of chlorine from the burning of old, insulated copper wire left the air rank. During that time, my morning class was World Civilization and I read my textbook every chance I got by the glow of that 50,000-pound blast furnace. I was paid $3.10 an hour and was grateful for the opportunity.

As a result, if any person has the right to write this book, it is I. I have seen it, I have experienced it, and I have overcome it. You will too, if you just give it half a chance.

This chapter is the last thing I have written for this book. I did not want to do it. It is painful and embarrassing. Many of my closest friends do not know these things about me. I did not even tell you the most gruesome things I have had to endure in my life. Some things are just too painful to recount. However, I hope I have shared enough of my story to convince you that someone who has actually been in the mire and muck of life wrote this book. I came out of that cycle of dysfunction and disappointment. You can too.

I have also written this book with a sense of urgency. I wanted to do one last good thing before I die. I have developed congestive heart failure and my kidneys are only functioning at 14 percent efficiency. Instead of pushing blood through my body, my heart is beginning to balloon. I have diabetes. One eye is blind and the other eye is at about half strength. The neuropathy is so bad in my hands that I have typed this entire book with just two fingers and a thumb. You see, I do have the "make-up gene."

That is all good. I am not afraid to die. In the past, I was afraid to die and not have my life count for something. This book may well be my legacy, my magnum opus. I am giving something back to the cosmos. I hope this book and the truth contained within it will aid you in your life journey. I believe this book and my story can show you a greater vision of the man you can become.

Read on, because I am one of you. I have *earned the right* to say these things to you.

Live well and fulfill your potential, my brothers,

Art

3. I Can Predict Your Future

I am writing to you because there are people who love you and they are concerned for you. They realize you have untapped potential. They see what you could become in life. One of those people may have given this book to you, in the hope that you will take a long, hard look at yourself by reading it. They feel there are issues in your life that are holding you back and keeping you from reaching your full potential as a man.

Your future:

If you don't confront the issues that are holding you back from realizing the full potential for your life, I can give you an accurate picture of how you will turn out in life. I may not hit it with 100 percent accuracy, but I will be frighteningly close.

Let me show you by letting you see through the looking glass of time. I have a good friend, named Bill, not his real name, who is now over sixty years old. His nickname is "Santa Claus Bill" because of his bushy white beard. Bill is a wonderful man. He will readily go out of his way to do anything for anyone. He is very involved in his church. The young men and women of his church adore him. He takes people fishing and helps the old folks in the church. The older men of the church seek his advice readily. His only vice is a serious addiction to rocky road ice cream and trail mix. He is in good health and is very fit and toned. People just love Bill.

So what is the problem, you may ask? Well, Bill is facing retirement with bleak prospects. He will survive, but Bill will probably struggle financially until he dies. At a time when he should be anticipating retirement years, during which he would be able to live comfortably on the accumulated resources from his long years of work, he has no savings or pension. He has no assets. Bill accepts this as his lot in life, but he knows now it could have been different for him.

What happened?

Bill experienced great physical and emotional abuse as a child in a very dysfunctional family structure. At a very young age, in an effort to cope with all the chaos around him, he vowed never to have anything, so it could not be taken away from him; never to love, so no one could ever hurt him; and never to strive too much for success, so he could not possibly fail. Bill shut himself away from fulfilling his true potential.

Bill got his wish. This life-changing decision, made long ago to protect his heart and soul, became the theme of his life. He spent many years in the military but opted out of the service before he secured a military pension. He obtained education in a number of fields, but he never established himself in any profession. He has loved and lost many times, but he regrets never having found his true-life companion.

Bill would have been a great father and grandfather. Even now, he makes plans to get his life up to speed, but he cannot seem to follow through to make better things happen. Did I tell you that Bill is a great guy? That's very true, but Bill acknowledges that the decisions he made so many years ago have really messed him up.

Bill gave me permission to tell you his story. His hope is that you will learn from it. Bill hopes his story will empower you to transform yourself into a man of fulfilled potential. If he were sitting across from you right now, he would say this:

> Don't be like me. I knew the unresolved issues in my life held me back. I have paid an awful price by not dealing with them. The things I was capable of would astound you, but somehow I didn't feel

I was worthy of success. You are young; there's still time for you to re-write the script of your life.

You can still have it all—a good career, a family who loves and respects you, peace in your mind, and happiness in your soul. Don't let the things other people did to you be the determining factors of your future. Don't let "them" make life decisions for you. Confront what happened, acknowledge how it has stalled your life, find the resources you need to overcome the troubling messages about yourself that are lodged in your head, develop a plan to overcome the hurdles you can't seem to clear right now and work your plan!"

Hear me when I say this: procrastination—putting things off until tomorrow—will suck the life right out of you.

Bill has broken the generation-to-generation cycle. He did not pass on the messages of low self-esteem to his children because he did not have any children. He broke the cycle by sacrificing his goals and true potential. He now knows that it was not the best option for his life. It certainly was not what God intended for him. Bill knows he has missed fulfilling his full potential. His experience tells him that.

However, experience is wasted on old men. By the time they get the experience, they are too old to do anything worthwhile. You can stay in the spot you now find yourself, but always remember Bill. He is you in forty years. Does that encourage you to let life pass you by? Or might Bill's true story serve to wake you up, kick you square in the butt, and motivate you to find the Real Man you were meant to be?

May God bless you for your efforts, should you decide now is a good time for a fresh start. May the power of His Son encourage you to do the work of analysis, healing, and rebuilding in your life; and may God's Holy Spirit lead you down the path of discovery, growth, and development that you will need to achieve your true potential.

We need good men, Real Men, in a new army, ready to change the world. The world desperately needs your talents and strengths. Your parents want the best for you, and even more than they were able to achieve for themselves. Your wife is longing for the man she loves to be whole, healthy, and happy. Your children do not want to share their daddy with the ghosts of the distant past any longer. The men and women of commerce are seeking young men they can promote to take over the reins of their businesses. Fight the good fight. The army of Real Men needs someone just like you, but whole, healthy, and realizing his full potential.

Do I have your attention?

Let's begin.

4. A Ten-Million Man Army

TEN MILLION: That is a big number. Imagine ten million of anything. Ten million men would be the largest army ever. You may be one of ten million young men estimated to be a part of the "lost generation." See if any of this hits close to where you live:

- You are unemployed or underemployed, and it is no big deal.
- You struggle with relationships. You love them, abuse them, and cannot understand why you lose them.
- You burn through money with great ease, and somebody always seems to bail you out.
- You are always making plans but never accomplishing much, because it is fun to chart your imaginary future, isn't it?
- You do not want to be bothered with all that "church crap" because God has never bothered with you before.

- You are not happy deep inside and you cannot even talk about it.
- You are angry with everybody, about everything, and believe the world is wrong.
- You are lonely in a crowd, because everybody else is so phony.
- You overcompensate to cover up feelings of inadequacy, because you can never let anyone know what an empty shell you are.
- You self-medicate with drugs and/or alcohol to feel normal, or just to feel something.
- You eat too much and you do not really know why, but food comforts you.
- You keep taking foolish risks just to feel something because you have accepted that when your number comes up, it is time to check out.
- You feel unfulfilled, and you cannot remember the last time you felt good about an accomplishment.
- You don't feel rewarded or affirmed as a man, because someone is always treating you like a kid.
- People (parents, bosses, friends, or women) always seem disappointed with you, and you do not believe they have the right to judge you.

- You have trouble articulating your feelings, so why bother.
- Deep inside there is fear and worry.

Do not blow this off!

You have started reading this for a reason. If any of the above picked off a scab in your mind, have enough respect for yourself to "man up" about it. There is an army of your fellow brothers waiting for some answers to jumpstart their lives. Join them! Like you, they are looking for answers that will give them a real reason to embrace life and fulfill their true potential as vital, purposeful men of accomplishment. Imagine what kind of impact an army of ten million men could have if they knew what it took to transform themselves into men of strength and purpose. Imagine what would happen if you put that knowledge into practice! Think of the possibilities. Your wife would have a brand new, cool man to love. Your kids would finally be in full possession of their daddy, the most important man in their lives. You unmarried guys would have women camping on your front lawn. Your friends would not recognize you. Business opportunities would emerge to ensure your advancement in your chosen career. It might get interesting.

I want to get gritty with you. I am not here to hold your hand or give you a little trophy for having a pulse. My job is to wake you up to a new vision of yourself. I was a pastor, but do not let that fool you. I can still kick butt without any problem! You must see what you are missing and what you could become as a fulfilled man, living up to your full potential, a Real Man.

Become a man of "Steel and Velvet":

I do not know many people who dislike Abraham Lincoln. Lincoln has been exalted as the quintessential man of "steel and velvet."[1] That is not my term, but it is a good one. Old Abe could also kick butt when he had to. He kept the nation from fragmenting at a crucial time in American history. Yet, he was known as a gentle man. He knew how to make plans and how to see those plans through to completion.

---

1   Aubrey P. Andelin, *Man of Steel and Velvet* (Santa Barbara: Pacific Press, 1972. The initial development of the concept is the work of Aubrey P. Andelin. I have used his initial work as a springboard to further develop the concept of the "Real Man."

Lincoln had acquired a sense of his own self-worth as a young man. That self-worth gave him purpose and the focus he needed to deal with the burdens he faced in his personal and public life. He could have made excuses that he had insufficient schooling, he had a headstrong wife, or that he had lost two sons due to disease and death. Instead, he accepted his challenges, overcame them, and fulfilled his potential. He was respected and people often sought his opinion.

When was the last time anyone sought your opinion over something crucial to life?

Lincoln is a good example of a Real Man, a man of "steel and velvet," who you might emulate as we mobilize this army of young men. Many men in history could serve as examples. They are worthy of study and imitation:

- George Washington
- Martin Luther King, Jr.
- Gandhi
- George Washington Carver
- John Wesley
- Booker T. Washington
- General George Patton
- General Dwight Eisenhower
- A guy named Jesus of Nazareth

These are just a few examples of noteworthy men. Such men come from all races, cultures, and countries. They can serve as examples and mentors who can still teach us lessons about life and what it takes to be a Real Man.

There are examples of men who were strong "men of steel" but who were lacking in good moral values, concern for others, or compassion. Consider Hitler, Stalin, Pol Pot, and Idi Amin. Look them up.

There are also examples of men who were all "velvet" and no "steel." History never records them, because they did nothing noteworthy. They may have lived their lives without killing anybody, but they did not achieve their true potential as Real Men.

Is there a Real Man in your life already, a man of both steel and velvet? Is there someone present for you to observe and emulate (copy, or become like)? Learn about him. Ask him if he would be willing to be a mentor to you.

Remember, the goal of all this is to develop an army of men who are in command of resources for development and growth, and who demonstrate right choices in their lives.

So, what does this man of "steel and velvet" look like?

Let us describe the fully formed man, the Real Man. This is the man God intended that all men become. Rest assured none of us ever achieves Jedi status in every facet of our lives. That is not possible. The goal is growth, development, and progress toward the actualization of our potential. Actualization is the increasing attainment of principles, objectives, goals, and skills within one's own life. There are the psychological, spiritual, educational, and behavioral dimensions to actualization.

Someone once said, "We are not called to be perfect; we are called to be faithful." Never forget that. With that in mind, let us unveil the Real Man.

The Real Man exists in four complementary parts.

The following descriptions are inspired and adapted from the book *Man of Steel and Velvet*. (See footnote 1.)

The strength (steel) of the Real Man is as follows:

- He accepts and assumes his duties as a man.
- He has a sense of pride in those duties.
- He works for the good of society.

- He is a man's man, not a wimp. He is not a macho he-man. He is a strong, sturdy, and dependable man.
- His character and behavior are above criticism at all times.
- He is optimistic about his life and his future.
- He is confident in his ability to care and provide for his family and himself, and He demonstrates the above characteristics behaviorally, because it is follow-through. He does not expect others to do this for him.

The soft dimension (velvet) of the Real Man contains these facets:

- He is gentle to women, children, the weak, and animals.
- He is tender even in situations requiring the use of his masculine strength.
- He is always kind.
- He is generous with his time and assistance.
- He is patient with others even in stressful situations.
- He is chivalrous, treating others with care and respect. He puts the needs of others above his own needs.

- He is attentive, observant, and anticipatory.
- He is respectful.
- He is always humble and never arrogant.

Softness is not weakness when combined with strength.

There is a third component of the Real Man. I call it mature "boyishness:"

- He can relate to youth, because there is still a little bit of the "boy" in him.
- He has a healthy, mature sense of playfulness.

Last, is the developmental component of the Real Man:

- He utilizes resources for skill enhancement, intellectual growth, psychological education and healing, and the nurturing of his mind and spirit.
- He seeks the help of competent mentors and professionals as the need arises.
- He sees the value of resources, such as reading, prayer, worship, study, and training to improve his life, and he uses them to achieve his full potential.

- He has a deep respect for education and he eagerly engages in lifelong learning.
- He never settles for mediocre achievements.
- He develops a sense of the "God-incidence," a divinely inspired coincidence meant to make him grow in potential as a Real Man. This is because he has a sense that all things will work together for his good, if he is open to such a possibility.

Look at these lists. You can become quite a guy!

What an army this will be and what transformation will take place in society! Imagine yourself as one of ten million men, achieving your full potential in your career, with your relationships, as a husband and dad, and as a fully realized individual. Imagine the peace and joy you will attain as you let the baggage of your past drop away. Imagine finding healing, wholeness, and purpose in your life. This will create a surge in societal growth never before experienced. What an army this could be and what a transformation there would be across the land.

In the next chapter, we will expand on the components listed above. You will begin to do some self-analysis and see where that takes you. You will begin your training as a soldier in the ten million-man army. You may see some God stuff thrown in here and there. Use what you need, not merely what you like. Okay, soldier, press on.

Mark 8:32 "You shall know the truth and the truth will set you free."

5. Taking the First Step

We have just finished showing you the Real Man. He is quite impressive, isn't he? He is always growing and developing his skills. He says what he will do and does what he says. He is in dynamic balance, because he works on the intellectual, physical, emotional, and spiritual dimensions of his life. His relationships are stable and long term. He is admired and respected. He is one powerful man!

You are going to answer some questions. They will begin to create your personal profile. Answer truthfully. There are no right answers; the answers will be specific to your history, attitudes, strengths, and challenges.

Question 1:

In what ways do you think you resemble the ideal Real Man?

(Answer in the space provided or use separate paper.)

Steel components:

Velvet components:

This question was designed to test your ability to see yourself objectively. To check if you see yourself realistically, share your responses to the above questions with someone who knows you well and who will be bluntly honest with you. Do not argue with them; just hear them. You have to find out how you recognize the real you and how others perceive you.

Art Heemer with Marilyn Wilson Miller and Sharon Lilly Runyon

Question 2:In what ways do you wish you were more like the Real Man?

There is the goal.

You have just identified some areas for growth and development. This is excellent. Remember them. You will need to write them down in your notebook later.

You want the differences between you and the Real Man to diminish over time. I do mean time, plus some real effort. You have to analyze who you are and exactly what is holding you back from your full potential. You need the chance to determine how willing you are to make the effort for the long haul. You cannot achieve things of real value without solid, sustained effort. So what is all this analysis and effort worth to you: more money, a happy wife and family, proud parents, career success, the joy and peace of accomplishment? You pick. I have already made the choices in my life. I have already done my work. Now it is your turn.

The point is that nothing comes from wishing and hoping.

Life is in the doing.

You are about to begin the process of re-making yourself.

The first step is to see yourself objectively, as others see you, and more importantly, discover what God sees for your life.

Are you still with me?

Good!

Are you at the place where you are ready to begin making some positive changes in your life? Have you had enough of your current situation?

If the answer is yes, then read on.

If your answer is no, give this book to someone who is ready for happiness, peace of mind, joy, and fulfillment. Always remember my friend, Bill. I cannot change you—that is your job. I can only give you a track upon which to run.

Here are some things to ponder and some things to begin to do. Get your pencil ready. Nobody is worthless. Surprise, this includes you!

1. **Write down your strengths as a man**
    (Your skills and things you do well)

2. Refer to the earlier lists describing the man of "steel and velvet")

   Identify the behaviors you exhibit that may lead others to suspect you are part of the "lost generation" of Gen X and Y men who are not fulfilling their true potential.

   Question 1 and 2 may sound like a repetition of the two previous questions, but you should answer them after you have shared your previous responses with another person. This will determine if you see yourself more clearly or if you are still being pig-headed about all of this self-analysis. Honesty is a good thing.

3. What would you like to improve upon in your life?

(Refer to the earlier lists describing the man of "steel and velvet.")

Here, you are beginning to address issues in your life that could use some tweaking.

This next question may be painful, in the emotional sense. Face this now and half the battle will be won.

4. **What are the things that still rattle around in your head, hold you back, divert your motivation, inhibit you from fulfilling your potential, or cripple you psychologically?**

    (These could be; childhood events, hurts, feelings of inadequacy, people with whom you are angry, relationships that ended badly, poor choices, etc.)

    Do not hold back here. Time to man-up and face what has controlled you until now. Write about what is bugging you.

    This question taps into the things that reside at the mental, psychological, or spiritual levels of your interior self. The issues you have identified will require sustained effort, possibly with a trained professional. Do not make that face at me! You would go to a trained professional to get a haircut, fill a cavity, or have your appendix removed.

5. What is your education level? How far have you gone in school?

In this question, I wanted you to become aware of what kind of a "tool chest" you have built up in your life so far. If you do not possess many "tools," then your career prospects may be crippled. Knowing what you have will lead to decisions about where you need to improve in this area of your life. Deciding what to do will be the crucial behavior for you, your future, and your family.

6. **What are you trained to do?**
    What have you trained yourself to do?
    What are you good at doing?
    What do you enjoy doing as work?
    ("Nothing at all" is not a valid answer!)

Here, you need to develop a sense of your marketability in the business world. There is not much call for pizza taste testers. One of the biggest assets a man has is his ability to trade his knowledge and skills for money. That is cold and bluntly capitalistic, but it is also deadly true. The only thing the world owes you is a shot.

7. What would you like to do as a career? What would be your ideal career?
(See previous parenthetical note.)

Your response to this question will indicate how realistically you are analyzing yourself. Delusions of grandeur will not be tolerated. I once knew a young man who wanted to be a video game programmer. He had zero college, hated math, and could not stay away from weed. He kept insisting that creating video games was the only job for him. Who was being scammed? By the way, he is now much older and no closer to his "dream job." He is delivering pizzas part time!

8. **List the significant relationships in your life today. For each relationship you list, answer the following questions:**
   Who is the person?

   Can you see any trouble spots? What are they?

   What is your fault in those trouble spots?

   Is that person worth fighting for, or are you willing to lose the relationship?

Remember the phrase "no man is an island." While you are living your life, you are also affecting the lives of countless people around you. Your lack of motivation, purpose, and direction are bad enough, if the only one being crippled is you, but your present situation is pulling down others as well. You are possibly having a bad effect on the woman in your life, your kids, your parents, your friends, your co-workers, and even the company where you work. Your growth and happiness will have a definite ripple effect outward. Think about that. Maybe there is a real issue requiring work, buried in all this relationship stuff.

9. How do you get along with others?
This can relate to friends, women, children, parents, neighbors, fellow workers, bosses, and others you encounter in a typical day.

Do you like them, or do you want to get a machine gun and "mow 'em down"?
(That was not a suggestion, by the way!)

Here is the relationship dynamic again! Question 9 deals a bit more with the larger world around you. A Real Man moves comfortably through the community and in his interactions with others. A Real Man is always cutting people a lot of slack.

10. Who do you admire in life?

I am speaking of a man, an example of a Real Man, with whom you can talk, and someone who would take your call.

Question 10 will show you if you can pick out the qualities of a Real Man when you see them in others. We are not talking about rich or famous here.

11. **How is your relationship with God?**

Are you on speaking terms? Are you scratching your head and muttering "God who?"

Are you "ticked off" at God?

(That is okay. He can take it. You are not the first and you will not be the last.)

Where do you go to recharge your spiritual dimension?

(Church, prayer, reading, music, art, hobbies, altered states of consciousness, etc.)

Finally, with this question I want you to ponder whether you feel there is anything outside your five senses, anything divine or supernatural. Is this life a dress rehearsal for a next life? What if that next life is dependent upon how well you mastered the skill-set assigned to you in this life? I'm just saying...

If you just did that little exercise quickly, I would bet the bank you did it poorly. That is okay. I did not give you any specific directions, did I? Since you probably have a raging headache now, take a break.

Put this book down and do not touch it for at least twenty-four hours.

I want you to ponder what you just wrote. I want you to percolate. I want you to stew in your own juices for a while.

Why?

Because you must do this part correctly, if you want to isolate those issues on which you need to begin work.

Okay, now put the book down!

I will see you tomorrow.

It is tomorrow. Why are some of you wearing the same clothes as yesterday? That must mean ... *the same underwear*! I am just kidding!

I want you to go through the above self-analysis again. You will find things to add. Do it. Slow down this time. The first round exposed the issues that were in the front of your mind. Now we are going to dig a bit deeper, because you have had time to let it percolate.

Neither today's nor yesterday's discoveries are more important than the others are. It is funny how the mind works. That twenty-four-hour period will prove to be very important, if you did any pondering at all. If you filled up the pages, use more paper.

Come back to this spot when you have finished the second run-through.

Wow! Look at you!

- You have identified and acknowledged your strengths.
- You have admitted and defined your weak areas.
- You have named and listed the issues that keep you from being in top form as a Real Man.
- You have begun to tap into what you are prepared for in your career and what train-

ing you may need to accomplish your career goals.

All of this is helpful to you. The analysis is specific to you. Nobody did his exactly the way you did yours. That is the beauty of this exercise; it does not try to make everybody the same. Our goal is to empower young men to become unique examples of the Real Man.

Are you ready for more?

My Ph.D. curriculum exposed me to the concept of testing and measurement. I learned how to create questionnaires and how to ensure the questions tapped into what required measurement. I also learned about "the magic number 7, plus or minus 2." What that phrase means is that people can only process from five to nine bits of information effectively at any given time. That is why the best billboards have no more than nine words in their ad copy. With this information in hand, I have developed a self-report testing instrument, which may put things in clearer focus for you. These five simple questions will give you a good snapshot of yourself. With the above exercise fresh in your mind, please answer the following questions. Your responses will range from 1 to 10 for each question. For each question, circle the number that best describes your opinion. Be honest, please, or else you will not have a valid measurement of your unique profile.

1. My childhood was:
Great   Very Rough

      1 2 3 4 5 6 7 8 9 10

2. I am:
Happy most of the time   hardly ever happy

      1 2 3 4 5 6 7 8 9 10

3. My relationships:
Are positive and carefree   are a train wreck

      1 2 3 4 5 6 7 8 9 10

4. My future:
Looks promising   looks bleak

      1 2 3 4 5 6 7 8 9 10

5. When faced with a problem or challenge:
I deal with it   I avoid it

      1 2 3 4 5 6 7 8 9 10

What this test shows about you:
Your responses on this five-question survey highlight the areas you may wish to work on initially. Any response marked higher than 5 is a valid issue for reflection and change. Let's go through them individually.

Question 1 addresses childhood or past history issues that may be holding back your full development as a mature man. These things are probably not your fault, but you need to address and conquer them. This is an area where a trained professional will be of great assistance to you. I personally prefer professionals who use the "Rogerian" counseling technique. They rephrase your questions and comments back to you in their own words, so you know that they understood you. There is nothing worse than a counselor who does not understand the issue you raise and is just talking because he likes the sound of his voice.

Question 2 addresses your moods and disposition. If you are experiencing more sadness, anger, and frustration than satisfaction, peace, joy, and happiness, then your outlook on life is the issue that you must address. This could mean some tweaking of your personal psychology, or even your spiritual perspective. I do not mean you have to become a "holy roller," but you do need to give some attention to the techniques you might employ to give your internal self some balance and perspective. Again, a trained professional would be a valuable resource. Real Men use resources that will help them grow and develop.

Question 3 addresses how well you get along with other people, and how they react and relate to you. Loved ones such as the women in your life, your children, and your friends can be an asset or a tremendous liability, depending on how great an investment they are willing to make toward your welfare, encouragement, and support.

Question 4 addresses your perception of how you view your prospects for a rewarding, successful, and meaningful life. If you cannot envision a successful life journey, you will need to find resources, develop skills, and learn techniques to confront and eliminate those roadblocks. A job counselor will definitely help with this issue. Additional education may be required with a response greater than 5 on this question. Some of you are skittish about more education because you hated high school. Adult education is not like that at all. Anything is easy to learn if you are interested in the topic. I had courses I hated and never did well in them.

Question 5 addresses issues of avoidance, procrastination, and accepting your role as a man. Some people delude themselves into the false premise that they can avoid making decisions indefinitely. They do this for weeks, months, and years. Finally, they realize their lack of decision *was* a decision, and life has passed by them. Living a "coulda, woulda, shoulda" lifestyle is pitiable to watch.

These two exercises are not difficult. Do not get all depressed and bent out of shape over what you have discovered. Acknowledge your strengths and admit your issues. These exercises will allow you to jot down five to ten or more areas you need to address and strengthen. Now you have a clearly defined track upon which to run. This knowledge will make it easier to re-mold yourself into your unique version of the Real Man.

That's great! Some people live their whole life and never come to an awareness of who they really are and what they might become. We applaud your efforts and honesty. We hope you feel some relief in this new knowledge about yourself.

We now know how to proceed with your boot camp, soldier. In the next chapter, we will begin.

Psalms 139:14 "I will praise You God; for I am fearfully and wonderfully made: marvelous are Your works; and that my soul knows right well."

6. Basic Training

Where should we begin? Since this may seem like the equivalent of boot camp, we could shave your head, make you wear ugly clothes, feed you garbage three times a day and psychologically beat you down...

However, to some of you, it would not be much of a change. Instead, we will go another way.

You are about to begin reconstructing your entire being, body, mind, attitudes, beliefs, values, and motivation. You will have to consider doing some things in sequence, consistently and with intention. They are:

1. Decide which things you want to address first, second, third, but no more at the beginning.

If you try to address everything at once, you will complete nothing. You will suffer information overload and your eyeballs will glaze over. Pick three things to work on. Write them down. Keep that list with you at all times. You can put them each on an index card, tucked in a convenient pocket. Refer to the list three times daily. Consult the list whenever a major decision comes your way. Begin to act and react based on how your behavior will enhance or inhibit those three issues. When you have those three under control, you can move on to the next three items. If you make a poor judgment, address the error and get back on track immediately.

What should you consider initially? The first three things should be important to you and not too overwhelming. Remember, we crawl before we walk; we walk before we run. Consider the following suggestions. You may want to order your unique list of things to address by rank (e.g., 1, 2, 3). As you read the following list, you may wish to build your "Personally Specific" list on a sheet of paper in a dedicated notebook for your "Growth and Development" or individually on 4" X 6" index cards. You will probably think of things unique to you that we cannot even imagine.

- Start a modest exercise program for twenty minutes a day. I would suggest a brisk walk for twenty minutes a day. You will need to sweat a bit and elevate your heart rate. Do not go all Godzilla here.
- Take off some weight. Start with two pounds a month. Small things can really

add up. Cut back on fast food, sweets, sugary drinks, and snacks. I said cut back, not eliminate. No one wants to starve you. Eat more fresh foods and unprocessed food items. Not everything is supposed to be fried, and salty, you know. You will feel less sluggish and have more energy and stamina. Do not ever give up pizza. Try to make it healthier!

- Seek out a group like Alcoholics Anonymous, Celebrate Recovery, or Gateway. You will learn you are not alone. You may find new friends who are working on their issues, too.
- Find a mentor who is a successful model to follow. Imitation is a powerful learning tool. He should be a good example of a Real Man.
- Seek out a trained counselor. If your history has you locked down, you need to respect your place in God's plan enough to seek a skilled professional. You can use the Yellow Pages, or ask your doctor. A pastor will have information on resources. You will want a stranger here as a counselor, not your pastor. Community agencies can give you referral information, too.

- Obtain your GED, or resume your college work. You cannot develop your assets and achieve your career goals without credible certification. The world does not care about your video game skills. They want to see transcripts, diplomas, and certification. Flipping burgers will not give you and your family security. Attain your full measure of achievement.

- Cut way back on the couch potato lifestyle. Try cutting back to 50 percent. You are better than that. Couch potato is not a good career choice.

- Back away from friends who are dragging you down. People in groups tend to sink to the lowest common dummy. Find people who cause you to stretch your horizons. They will make you a better person.

- Go find a church and see how many older people faint when you show up. The opportunities for growth may surprise you.

- Sit down with your wife, girlfriend, or mother and tell her about your determination to do this thing. It will be helpful to have someone supportive in this with you. Tell her you welcome encouragement, but will not appreciate heavy, negative criticism.

- Check for a support group or a men's group in your area. The networking will help keep you on target. Accountability to others is a great motivator.
- Make a 30-60-90 day list of goals and objectives for change and growth, and actually implement it. The 30-day goals should lead to the 60-day goals, which should lead to the 90-day goals. There is no use considering this if you are not going to use it to change your behavior.
- Write some yearly goals down on paper, seal them in an envelope, and keep a copy to read. Write a date six months into the future on the sealed envelope to indicate when to open it to check your progress. I would do this periodically with my chosen mentor. If you achieve all your goals, that is great! If you do not achieve some of them, do not get suicidal. Those unrealized goals just go at the top of the next set of goals.
- Tell the people in your life, whom you have disappointed, about your plans for growth and development. Apologize for past errors, if you need to. That will give you a clean start.
- Switch from alcohol to coffee. Coffee stimulates and alcohol depresses. Trust me:

you are not a barrel of laughs when you are drunk and depressed. Never, never use illegal drugs. (Do I *really* have to mention this?)

- Seek out a career counselor. He might be able to turn your lame career idea into something actually worthwhile.

- Visit some non-college training programs to see if they might help you to attain your career goals. Not everybody needs a four-year college degree. There are excellent two-year and trade/technical degrees that lead to excellent careers.

- Make a budget and use it. There are many budget websites on the Internet. You can write it in a notebook, or use Word or Excel on a computer. The goal of a budget is to track where your money goes and then to distribute that money to cover bills and obligations. Here is a great tip: live on 90 percent of your income and *always* save 10 percent. You will thank me for this. I know you will!

- Save $10 a week in a savings account and do not touch it until it is at least $500. Do not blow it on crap!

- Pay more attention to your grooming, hygiene, and clothing. You really need to be healthy, clean, and not smell like a two-legged cat box.

You get the picture. We have probably missed a hundred additional things for you to consider. Make it your program. The first three items you pick will take at least ninety days of consistent effort to begin to feel like ingrained habits. Do not add a fourth item before ninety days, otherwise it will bog you down. Master those three things on your list and then move on. Change may start slowly, but as you get more skilled at living like a Real Man, things will start to speed up. It is referred to as the "practice effect."

2. Re-arrange your time to work on your issues agenda.

Face it: you are here because when the events and situations happened that got you to this place, the time and resources you invested to address the problems you encountered were not enough. Now you are hauling a 400-pound gorilla around on your back. He is breathing down your neck, and he stinks! You need to get him off your back or learn to love him. You have to re-allocate sufficient time to see the effects of your effort. This effort may require some money for supplies: stamps, a notebook, some index cards, phone calls, etc. Wishing and hoping will accomplish nothing. I suggest you allocate fifteen hours a week for growth and development activities. This will become your new hobby. You will spend some time (1) reflecting on where you are heading in life, (2) listing what issues you need to work on most immediately, (3) strategizing your growth behaviors, (4) and implementing those strategies. Fifteen hours a week is about two hours a day. It is a comfortable time allotment. It will give you plenty of time for the rest of your daily responsibilities. This can be "scrap time," while you are on a coffee break, waiting for the laundry to finish, or while waiting for the wife to finish her "girly stuff" instead of yelling at her to hurry up. You get the idea.

3.   Don't even *try* to do this alone.

Here comes the God stuff. The Creator of the universe had perfection and the fulfillment of your potential in mind when He created you. The book of Psalms says, "I am fearfully and wonderfully made." Another line in the book written by Jeremiah says, "For I know the plans I have for you," declares the Lord, "plans to prosper you and not to harm you, plans to give you hope and a future." Does it not make sense that if God spent all this effort making you fully capable of reaching your true potential, He just

Art Heemer with Marilyn Wilson Miller and Sharon Lilly Runyon

might interact with you in real time to make it happen?

You can talk with Him any time you want. Just talk. You do not need fancy words or special formulas. Just talk. You do not even have to close your eyes. They didn't in the ancient days. (Don't tell the preacher; he will have a stroke!) Just talk. Tell God what is keeping you down. Ask Him to forgive anything that is your fault. Ask His Son to come abide in your life and help you live like a Real Man. Finally, ask Him to send His Holy Spirit to lead, guide, and direct you to the *next right thing* in your life. Just ask!

Get that phrase into your head. The life of a Real Man is a series of *next right things.*

Today's next right thing is to pick three things that need improvement.

Tomorrow's next right thing is getting to work on those three things, and so on.

Once you start stringing days together, where all you do is the next right thing, you will notice a pattern of right living emerging from the ashes and despair of your current situation. That pattern is "righteous living." It is not yet holy living, but it is a start. Remember, baby steps.

If you ask for those things, God will hear you and He will respond. You may not be the trusting type. You may have never been able to trust

70

anyone. God dares you to put Him to the test. Go ahead and call His bluff. He will amaze you. Then you will amaze others.

Perhaps some of you were expecting a different type of book. I cannot provide you heavy psychological analysis or therapy here. If you need that, seek out a professional.

There is no such thing as a magic phrase or a magic pill to make everything better. If there were, this book would have cost a lot more. This book is designed for the guy who needs a kick in the pants, and who is in need of some general direction.

I believe most guys would be willing to sign on to a program of growth and development, that leads to Real Man status, if only they could make peace with the past and catch a powerful vision of who they could really be in this life. However, most guys aren't wired to see the subtle interactions between what they feel, what they do, and how it affects people and situations around them. For example, some guys can't quite make the leap between drinking a little too much beer and their wife not letting them near her for two weeks. They do not see the connection between having lived a life with no purpose or goals and the painful realization twenty years later that their children have no respect or use for them.

They do not understand the correlation between never setting money aside for the old men they will someday be and the stark reality of a retirement filled with sacrifice and deprivation. You can be brighter than that.

Behind every action, there is a psychology. Therefore, both attitudes and behaviors must change.

Your history, attitudes, beliefs, values, and concepts of "normal behavior" have shaped who you are today. The things you feel you need to change will not change until you modify your attitudes, beliefs, and values. Merely changing behaviors, without changing the underlying attitudes, beliefs, and values that drive the behavior is not sustainable. Ask any "dry drunk" who relapses. His behavior may have changed for a while. His attitudes never budged. The sooner you grasp that concept, the faster you will transform into a Real Man.

So what are attitudes, beliefs, and values? [2]

An attitude is a feeling, emotion, or an opinion that you hold about a person, thing, event, concept, or topic. It can change with data or proof that compels you to do so. For example, I have an attitude about the vegetable called okra. I do not like it. I do not think I should have to eat something that has a nasal condition. It has always been too slimy for my palate. However, I did have some breaded, baked okra that was surprisingly good once (I was trying to appear cool in the presence of a woman I was interested in dating). Since then I have had to adjust my attitude concerning okra. Attitudes can change rather easily, and logical reasoning does not always change them.

Beliefs are a little more entrenched. Think of them as attitudes on steroids. A belief is a firmly

---

2   Milton Rokeach, *Beliefs, Attitudes, and Values: A Theory of Organization and Change,* Jossey-Bass Behavioral Science Series, 1968. Rokeach was a pioneer in researching the concepts of attitudes, beliefs, and values. My discussion of the topic is a result of studying his work in graduate school. Rokeach fueled many graduate term papers, theses, and dissertations in the field of Communication research.

held judgment or conviction, which is supported by a whole cast of underlying attitudes, because beliefs are usually multi-dimensional in nature. For the belief to change, most if not all of the underlying attitudes that support the assertions of the belief must change. This change of belief can happen but rarely does. A good example might be when one changes political affiliation or switches to a different religious denomination. Most guys I've known who switch religious denominations do so because of a woman in their life, which is a whole different dynamic—it can sometimes be love but is usually lust!

A value is the most entrenched component of a person's core being. A value is a principle held to be intrinsically valuable or desirable. Attitudes and beliefs support values. Therefore, values are rarely altered because too many attitudes and beliefs would require re-arranging to change a value. A concept such as the sanctity of human life is the sum total of one's history, instruction, and training on the subject of human life, attitudes concerning the various facets of the subject, and the beliefs those attitudes give rise to. Think about values, such as the man as the primary breadwinner, man as the provider, man as the strong moral influence in a family, honesty, thrift, and perseverance. These are all values of a Real Man.

Opinions lead to attitudes, which lead to beliefs, which result in values.

Your job will be to ponder your attitudes concerning your issues. You will have to decide which attitudes are logically arrived at and helpful to your agenda of growth and development. "Does this attitude help me, or does this attitude hurt me?" If an attitude is bogging you down, you must alter it or drop it. Scrutinize those attitudes that serve to support your beliefs for logical consistency and value to your life and goals. Only worthwhile attitudes and beliefs will propel you toward Real Man status. Your beliefs, which are serving as the underpinnings of your value structure, must be fully compatible with those values. Inconsistency and poor logic at any level can be hindering and debilitating. In fact, I am willing to assert that a major component in your rebuilding process will revolve around attitudes, beliefs, and values that are poorly thought out, inconsistently formulated, and inappropriately utilized. This work may take a lifetime, and that is not necessarily a bad thing.

Following every action, there will be a consequence.

Modern conservative theology has warped our generation in this regard. Most people think that if they commit a wrong, they just have to pray about it and God will give them a "do over." He will forgive everything and life can go on. The problem is that the Bible does not teach that at all. There will always be painful consequences. Some consequences will be immediate, such as a lost job or the end of a relationship. While other consequences may pop up in the future, like, "This is little Bubba and I think you're the father. Open your mouth so we can get a DNA sample."

However, issues of accountability and consequence always need to be addressed. Forgiveness and accountability always go together. If you have a girlfriend or wife, you probably understand some things about being accountable for your actions a bit better now than you did when you were single. The same thing works with moms, dads, friends, employers, siblings, and even the law.

Those may be new concepts to you, but you had better get comfortable with them. A large percentage of the guys who are reading this stumble over the consequences of their actions. They do not call it "manning up" for nothing.

Cause and effect got you into this ditch, and using cause and effect will pull you out of this ditch.

Okay, if you just gotta' have a magic phrase, how about these two:

1. What you do today will cast ripples out into your life, the consequences of which you cannot even begin to imagine right now.
   This is the future implication. This applies to the good as well as bad things you do.
2. The things you do right now have been scripted by the events of your past and the attitudes, beliefs, and values you have acquired as a result.
   This is the past affecting your present behavior. The interior motivations always drive the exterior actions.

That is profound, man! Your journey and the success in your life are dependent upon achieving a dynamic balance and truce with the past, present, and future. Your former struggle to achieve Real Man status is a symptom that your past is fighting against your present and is negatively affecting your future.

Every college sophomore knows the whole world is interconnected. That is why they think they know everything! They do not, by the way. In your boot camp of growth and development, you will have to deconstruct yourself through analysis and reflection. You will then strategize the best plan of attack to address your problem areas, and implement that plan. There may be false starts. There may be failed attempts at change. That is normal and quite expected. Watch kids trying to learn to ride a two-wheeled bike. They try and they fall, try and they run into the bushes, try and they realize they never practiced turning or stopping, and finally try and they succeed. What kept them going? What urged them on and never let them give up? It was the vision of what they had not yet attained. When they mastered riding a two-wheeler, a new world opened up for them. There was a shift in their entire perspective of the world and its boundaries.

Do you get the connection here? Your life will make a quantum shift in perspective and the impossible will suddenly be attainable. Others have done this very thing. Now is your time.

Do you remember the mentor? He will be crucial, right now. Find him.

How to turn your life around step by step:

1. Get a notebook and a pen or pencil. In that notebook write down the information the earlier analysis told you about yourself. The first page will detail your strengths and good qualities. The second page will detail your weaknesses, challenges, and areas for growth and development. The third page will list the resource persons and groups you will want to initially contact. The fourth page will list 5–10 issues you have identified and want to consider focusing on. Rank order them (1, 2, 3, etc.) according to your evaluation of their importance. Number 1 would be the first issue for you to address, and so on.

2. On three index cards, write the first three issues you have decided to work on, one issue to a card. Those cards have just become like tattoos because they will never leave your person. You will refer to them every hour if you need to. Okay, you can put them on the back of the toilet when you shower. On the back of each index card, you will note the names, addresses, and phone numbers of your resources and mentor.

3. On the fifth page of your notebook, you will begin to develop a strategy for what you will do to address and conquer those three initial issues. You may find that the three issues are somewhat intertwined, so things you do concerning one issue may also affect the other two issues.

4. Now you work your plan—every day, all day, for ninety days. You will find that you may need to adjust your strategies, but this is no big deal. You will discover things you had not anticipated, still no big deal. The only big deal is not working your plan. Once the ninety days are over, decide if you can begin to address any new issues. If not, that is okay; keep working on the first three issues. When you can add a fourth issue to the mix, you will discover something. It will not be so difficult to strategize or implement change concerning the fourth issue. Again, that is the practice effect.

5. You will note that some issues are conquered, some are still in process, Periodically, every 6–12 months, go through the analysis and list your issues and some new issues may surface. This is both normal and desirable. This is a sign of growth, development, and progress.

6. If you currently have no use for God and spiritual things, ignore this (#6). However, if you see some benefit to seeking outside help in this project, you may use the prayers and reflections in Chapter 7, and embrace just a little bit of Bible reading (see #10 in chapter 8), and begin to read the ideas of great men in literature. You will definitely be ahead of the curve. These behaviors will supply you with ideas, tips, and techniques you might not ever acquire otherwise. You just might arrive at Real Man status years ahead of schedule.

It is that simple. Make a plan and work your plan. I would keep my notebook in a safe, private place. Other people do not need to read your stuff. I would be extremely careful about with whom I shared details. In addition, do not brag or get cocky! You are working on your issues, but you are not ready to give guest lectures yet. Along the way, you will need to attend to some education and nurture facets of your plan. When an opportunity for training comes your way, get a clue. If a gremlin or ghost from your past pops up, deal with it, hammer it, and do not build it a guest room. I predict you will begin to see movement in your life soon, and results will be evident quickly.

Four ninety-day cycles will amaze the people around you. The year is going to roll by whether or not you do this work. So you might as well do the work of becoming the Real Man.

I wish I could be beside each of you, instructing, cautioning, and screaming like a drill sergeant, but I cannot. Our work is done. The intent was not for this to be a lengthy book. Face it: guys don't read long books. We tried to keep things enjoyable and not too heavy, although this is serious business. It is your life. It is your future, your family's well being, your happiness, and your contentment we are discussing. We really hope you have made an honest decision to commit to the "man of steel and velvet" who is waiting to become *you*.

When you are old, like me, maybe you will be able to lift up the young men of the next generation. Those future young men will have issues to face just as you did. They will need mentors, coaches, and examples of Real Men as patterns to copy in their lives. If my effort here has sparked something in your spirit and if my concern for your wellness has caused you to begin this incredible journey, then the greatest honor you could give me is to "pay it forward." Tell those young men about a little book you once read, a book that caused you to re-evaluate who you were and what you could really become. I hope I will be able to check in on you from time to time, from where I will be.

In the last section of this book, you will find some reading resources to focus on specific areas of your growth and development. You will also be introduced to some prayers and reflections you might find useful. I wrote three of them just for you. My friend, Ramona, wrote the other one. In addition, there is a section with tips concerning research of these topics on the Internet. Lastly, there is a section entitled "Other Useful Stuff." It is a place for writing things for quick reference.

I have had some fun doing this project. Marilyn and Sharon have shared a few laughs with me, too. I have had the opportunity to reflect on my life journey toward Real Man status. I feel as if, in doing this project, I have finally paid a debt I owed to the mentors who patiently shepherded me in my formative young adulthood. Have I arrived completely? Others may answer that question more honestly. I am not what I always want to be; I am not what I ultimately will be; but thank God, I am not what I was! That is our wish for you, my brothers.

There is just one more thing I have to say.

Do not make me come back! Make us proud soldier.

Carry on.
Art, Marilyn, and Sharon

Hebrews 2:7–8 "You made him [man] a little lower than the angels; You crowned him with glory and honor, and did set him over the works of Your hands: You have put all things in subjection under his feet."

7. Prayers and Reflections

These are prayers designed just for you. Use them daily for at least thirty days. You may photocopy them in reduced form and laminate them, so they fit in your shirt pocket.

Morning Prayer (of sorts)

(Read this over breakfast every day.)
Okay, God, I'm up, already.

I do not want this to be a day that controls me; I want us, You and I, to make this day worth getting up for.

You claim all this power—well, I am going to need a bucket-full today.

As You track me, God...

1. When I screw up, kick me in the pants.
2. When I get it right, help me to know and be aware of it.
3. When people are in my face, give me the calmness not to rip out their hearts.
4. Make me comfortable with me, God.

5. Keep the vision of what I can fully accomplish today, and in my life, always in front of me.

6. Give me joy knowing You are here with me.

You have said in Your Book that I would be able to do all things through the power of Your Son, who will give me strength. Well, I am calling You on it, God. I am willing. Take over the controls. I do not want to crash and burn any more. Make me aware of Your hidden angels and helpers all around me, and make me smart enough to accept their help.

Keep the Devil's junk from leading me into trouble.

Give me a powerful saying to reflect upon this day.

It will be a good day—a wonderful day.

I will live like a man, a good man, a man of worth and power—Your man, God.

I am asking this in the name of Your powerful Son,

Amen (so let it be)

It's Lunchtime, Lord:

(Guys, this is your midday prayer.)

Here is my day so far, Lord

_____ I have had it good so far. Keep it up, God!

_____ I have imagined my boss horribly killed 30 times so far.

_____ That woman needs to stop flashing by me in that tight outfit.

_____ I am going to run that jerk over in the parking lot.

_____ I invented a new cuss word, God.

_____ That guy ate my lunch last week. It was just payback.

_____ Other

You know where my slippage is, God—I know it, too.

Forgive me and help me be stronger.

Holy Spirit of God, guide me to walk like a Real Man for the rest of the day.

Make me Your man, God.

Show more of You and less of me.

- Less of my arrogance
- More of Your wisdom
- Less of my foolish passions and appetites
- More of Your steadiness
- Less of my way and self-centered agenda

- More of Your will for making me that Real Man
- Less of my hateful opinions and actions
- More of Your love, showing through my life, God

It is a good thing You didn't call us to be perfect. I am glad You only called us to be faithful. Perfection is a process, I am learning.

So, keep polishing me, God. Knock down the rough places in my heart and in my life. Turn me toward the place called Faith, where men are wise and good. May others see that I am a good man—a Godly man. May they want what I have, Lord.

Make me humble enough to seek forgiveness where I have been wrong and make me wise enough for the rest of the day.

Again, I am asking You to provide the power in my life.

Amen (make it so, Number One)

It's Evening and About Time!

(Guys, this is the bedtime prayer.)
Well God, I made it—just barely.
Now I get to reflect on all the stuff of the day:

- The good things I did, and am proud of
- The embarrassing stuff
- The things I'm getting better at
- The things that still trip me up
- People I helped today
- People I hurt today

Please forgive my mistakes and the sins for which I am guilty. Help me not to repeat them. Keep me away from anything that makes me avoid my work toward being a better man each day. Show me strategies for a more successful tomorrow.

Give me a powerful verse from my reading in Your Bible that I can apply to my life right now. Make me read it slowly and carefully, so I can find all the resources for my growth as Your man.

Give me good, restful sleep. I give my problems to You tonight. I am tired of dealing with them, Lord. We will work on them again tomorrow.

Please give me peaceful sleep.
Thanks for all Your help today, God.

Signing off 'til the morning,
Amen (See you then, Lord—my "Loaf Giver"
of daily bread)

This one is Ramona Severn's prayer and reflection. We like it.

Ramona is a friend of ours. Her husband, Randy, also a friend, worked with me, Art, at United Parcel Service in South Bend, Indiana, when we were in college together (my best job while in college). They are phenomenal people and very devoted to one another. This reflection on Psalm 23 comes from the depths of Ramona's soul, as she valiantly cared for Randy during a serious illness and the resulting complications he developed. I am happy to say Randy recovered and they are deeper in love than before. If this does not stir your soul, check for a pulse.

Pondering 23 While Traveling 60 West at 4 a.m.

The Lord is my shepherd
- He devotes himself full time to watch over me.
- It is His only desire that I am cared for.
- If I wander or get lost, He will pursue me.

I shall not want.
- I need not worry or fret about my needs.
- I will be taken care of because I am being shepherded.

He maketh me to lie down

- He knows that I need rest.
- He wants me to take time to be refreshed.
- If I don't take the time to rest, He could possibly "make me" lie down.
- I may experience a time where things are taken out of my control.

in green pastures;
- He will lead me to where my needs will be met.
- He will provide a place where I can be comforted and relaxed.

He leadeth me beside the still waters.
- He leads the way. He doesn't drive me. I must choose to follow.
- He not only provides nourishment of food, but refreshing water to fill me and cleanse me inside and out; not turbulent, frightening water, but still, calm, safe water.

He restoreth my soul.
- This pastoral scene not only meets my physical needs, but provides beautiful restoration to my spirit.
- The Shepherd can restore what the worries, sufferings, abuse and rust of the world have damaged deep within me.

He leadeth me in the paths of righteousness

- If I will allow Him to lead me, He will guide me in the way that is right.
- It is not a broad highway, but a pathway.
- And why does He lead me?

for His name's sake.

- By following this path, His name will be glorified.

Yea, though I walk through the valley of the shadow of death,

- This path of rightness may not always be easy.
- It may at times be a dark valley, far from the mountaintop.
- It may seem like the walls are closing in around me.
- But this is not the valley of death.
- This is only the shadow of death.
- The follower of the Shepherd may have to pass through the shadow,
- But will not be consumed by the reality of eternal death. Therefore,

I will fear no evil;

- I have no reason to fear the shadow or the evil around me. Why?

for Thou art with me;

- because the Shepherd is with me in the valley, even in the shadow.

Thy rod and Thy staff
- The Shepherd may nudge me and push me in the right way, or discipline me for my own good and humility, making me more useful.
- He may rescue me from danger if I fall out of safety.
- The Shepherd will protect me from evil that may attack me.

they comfort me.
- These realities give me great comfort.
- Even though the valley, the shadow, death and evil are all around me,
- I can take comfort that He is with me, using His ways for my good.

Thou preparest a table before me
- The Lord will prepare a feast of provision in front of me...
- in the presence of mine enemies:
- even though there is opposition in my presence.

Thou anointest my head with oil;
- The Shepherd heals my wounds.

- He prepares and commissions me for specific tasks.
- He will use my wounds to help heal others.

my cup runneth over.

- All of this provision, comfort, guidance, restoration, protection, presence, discipline, pursuit, healing, and purpose causes me to have more than "just enough,"
- it provides plenty to spill over on to others who need...
- joy beyond description—overflowing.

Surely goodness and mercy shall follow me

- I am convinced that because of the Shepherd's love, His goodness will be close behind me, perhaps even following my days in the lives of those that I have touched.
- His compassionate mercy, His patient restraint of what I truly deserve will continue wherever I go because of His forgiveness,

all the days of my life;

- especially during this first chapter of my "life," which I number daily...

and I will dwell in the house of the Lord forever.

- But most gloriously in the eternal perfection of the incredible paradise in which He resides and offers to share with me for eternity.

Ramona Severn
Tampa General Hospital
August 2008*

---

* *While traveling the long, lonely road to Tampa at 4 a.m., transporting my slumbering, weakened husband to one of his weekly surgeries after eight months of battling cancer and infection.*

8. *Resources for Further Growth and Development*

Here is a list of resources for further reading and reflection. This is not a complete list. Consider it a starting point on your lifelong journey of reading, reflection, and growth. A Real Man is a literate man, always seeking and internalizing understanding and wisdom.

You may not find some of these resources in bookstores, so search the local libraries too. Used bookstores are another good way to find out of print books. They are worth the hunt.

Note: It is traditional to list references alphabetically. I have decided to forego this practice. I have listed the following either in the order that I used the resource in the writing of the book, or as I discovered the reference for inclusion into this list of resources (see 11 and 12). You will figure it out.

1. Daniel Jay Soukin, Ph.D. *Wounded Boys, Heroic Men.* Holbrook: Adams Media Corp., 1998.

This book is a resource for men who survived abuse as young children. It is comprehensive and well written. It contains extra help for the recovering and rebuilding young man. This is a resource I have always had in my professional library.

2. Aubrey P. Andelin. *Man of Steel and Velvet*. Santa Barbara: Pacific Press, 1972.

This book was the impetus for the descriptions of what characteristics the Real Man will possess. It goes into greater depth than we were able to cover in this book. It may be out of print, so check your library first. It is an especially good resource concerning man/woman relationships.

3. Sam Keen. *Fire in the Belly: On Being a Man*. Bantam Books, New York, 1991.

If you hate reading, read this book. Keen unwraps the male animal, peeling back layers of tradition, culture, myth, and psychology. You will understand "maleness" intimately when you finish. There is a very useful self-administered analysis in the back of the book.

4. Robert Moore and Douglas Gillette. *King Warrior Magician Lover: Rediscovering the Archetypes of the Mature Masculine*. San Francisco: Harper San Francisco, 1990.

This book examines the psychology of boys versus the psychology of men, their similarities and differences. It also discusses the myths, cultural pulls, stereotypes, and archetypes of the masculine male. It is for guys who are in the intermediate and advanced stages of rebuilding themselves.

5. Bruce Larson. *30 Days to a New You: Reprogramming Your Potential for Positive Purpose and Power-filled Living.* Grand Rapids, MI, Zondervan, 1994.

Men are not the only focus of this book. Both genders can use it, especially as a self-help resource for couples. Remember, guys, dysfunction breeds dysfunction. If you are in a relationship while you are working on growth issues, both partners will be in need of some fine-tuning. This book explores a person from God's perspective and God's intention. It is very spiritual, and only Real Men and committed couples should attempt this one.

6. Denis Waitley. *Seeds of Greatness: The Ten Best-kept Secrets of Total Success.* Old Tappan, New Jersey: Fleming H. Revell Company, 1983.

This book is the result of years spent studying people who are successful and happy to find the common traits they share. Each chapter unveils a different seed of greatness. It is phenomenal!

7. Dr. Wayne W. Dyer. *Your Erroneous Zones.* New York: Funk & Wagnalls, 1976.

This book exposes all the little gremlins that hold us back in life and teaches how to kill them systematically. The last chapter paints a portrait of what you will become if you eliminate your erroneous zones.

8. George D. Armerding, with Phil Landrum. *The Dollars and Sense of Honesty: Stories From the Business World.* New York: Harper and Row, 1979.

This is a classic book about ethics and honesty. Did you know that honesty could make you rich, and poor ethics can bankrupt you? It provides real-life examples.

9. Robert H. Schuller. *Be an Extraordinary Person in an Ordinary World.* Old Tappan, New Jersey: Fleming H. Revell Company, 1985.

Dr. Schuller lays out nine "Extraordinarys" that are crucial to a Real Man. This book is filled with real-life examples of extraordinary people who could be vicarious mentors for you.

10.The Holy Bible, by God (and a few helpers).

You may want to do some reading in a Bible. If it were my call, I would start with the book of

John in the New Testament, which you will find in the back half of the Bible. You might also read the book of Proverbs in the Old Testament, front half, which has some wise sayings to live by. The Psalms, located in the Old Testament, will give you stuff to ponder when you are troubled. In the New Testament, Galatians, Ephesians, and Philippians are letters written by a guy named Paul. They explain the Christian lifestyle pretty well. That is enough for a while.

About Bibles: This is just my opinion, but it is a studied opinion. I did a research project when I was in graduate school on the various translations and paraphrases of the Bible. Here is what I found.

There are those who say that the King James Version (KJV) of the Bible is the only pure version and that all other versions are tainted. Do not believe them! The KJV is hard to understand, and it is not true to the most ancient manuscripts in some places. If that is all you have, then use it. However, you would understand two other versions of the Bible more easily.

The Living Bible is a paraphrase, not an accurate translation. However, it reads easily and is very understandable. Guys who have never had much experience reading the Bible should enjoy its modern wording. It does have some translation errors, but you will not find them. I once lost two points on an exam in a Bible survey class by using it as my study Bible. The professor warned me and I didn't listen!

For my money, the most accurate Bible translation today is The New International Version (NIV). It is easy to read. If something has crept into the text of the Bible that was not found and supported by the ancient manuscript text documents, you will be told about it (and there are a few places like that ... not a big deal, but they are there.) The NIV is one of very few translations of the Bible that uses input from every known scrap of the ancient Scripture manuscripts. I respect the work of the researchers who translated out of Hebrew, Aramaic, and Greek. I cannot say enough good things about the NIV translation. I stand by my findings.

There is another new paraphrase of the Bible called *The Message.* I am not especially keen on it, because I fear it can lead to a cloudy perception of New Testament, and Christian doctrinal truths. Nevertheless, try it if you are curious.

11. John Eldredge. *Wild at Heart: Discovering the Secret of a Man's Soul.* Nashville: Thomas Nelson, 2005.

The aim of this book is to aid men in restoring their God-created passions. The book also discusses appropriate, God-approved risk taking.

12. Mark Driscoll and Gary Breshears. *Vintage Jesus: Timeless Answers to Timely Questions* (Relit Theology). Wheaton, IL.: Crossway/Good News Publishers, 2008.

This book brings Biblical authority and power to the questions being raised today in our culture.

9. Internet Resources

1. **Search terms:** Generation X, Generation Y, echo boomers, dysfunctional, the definitions of attitude, beliefs, and values, motivation.

2. **Budgets:** The Internet is full of budget Web sites. Some offer education and information on how to set up a budget. Others offer free budget planners, worksheets, and spreadsheets. If you are Excel literate, you can set up a budget that keeps track of weekly, monthly, quarterly, semi-annual, and yearly financial obligations. If you are good at Excel, you can get the spreadsheets to keep track of cash flow and warn you if you will not have enough money to cover expenses, so you can reallocate finances without getting over-extended.

3. **Education:** You can research career opportunities on the Internet. You can request information on educational programs and some sites even offer virtual tours of their

campuses. You can also research grants, loans, and other aid packages.

4. **Support groups:** Most regional and national support groups have a presence on the Internet. You can even hook up to them through Facebook and Twitter. Some groups offer online chat and counseling services. I would use the search terms of the particular issue you are interested in such as: alcohol dependence, drug abuse, childhood abuse, men's issues, depression, men's groups, overeating, underachievement, men's growth, etc.

5. **Relationships:** These resources may be harder to locate, but the exercise may prove fruitful. You know, counseling can be a great way to re-establish your love. I would not wait until the relationship was in deep trouble before I got concerned enough to seek help. There are seminars, weekend retreats, counselors, and therapists. These resources can make a bad relationship better and a good relationship phenomenal. There is nothing like a happy partner, buddy!

10. Other Useful Stuff

Use the following pages to help keep information in a convenient, accessible place. Write the information as you obtain it. I would use pencil on these pages, as you may wish to erase occasionally.

My mentor:

His phone number

His address

My resource group(s):

Name of group(s)

Web site(s)

Phone number(s)

Address(es)

Strengths I have discovered within myself:

Issues I have encountered that need to be addressed:

30-day goals:

60-day goals:

90-day goals:

Educational resources:

GED program/technical school/college name and phone number:

Contact person, phone number, and address

People to whom I need to talk:
(These can be resources, people to whom you need to apologize, or new people you have recently met on this growth and development adventure, and people you want to stay in touch with you.)

Names and contact numbers

Reading resources I want to investigate:
(Write them down so you will not forget.)

Miscellaneous items: